L.D.

MW00917675

Is there anything you wou... ...., -.,- - - g

Cronyk

Sure, all of the writings on this album I made with a purpose. These are my true emotions about the things occurring in communities nationwide. I have never been a bandwagon rider, so I can understand if you disagree with some of my views.

My intent is to inform some people and lead others to an answer that could solve our problems. If at any point you get offended by my perspective, please know from the bottom of my heart, I could care less. I am part of the HIP HOP generation. The generation of Americans that will stand and forever fight for the 1St Amendment "FREEDOM OF SPEECH." Welcome to The Interview.

The Interview

1. I was Westside born native to the Windy City
2. so that should let you know the life wasn't always too pretty
3. she's a trip that forever get to trippin
4. but the heart of the land kept me pushing through the gritty
5. I never fuss just play the cards that they deal me
6. say I heard at my birth that they really tried kill me
7. nah youngin you don't feel me
8. said I heard at my birth that they really tried killed me
9. mama on the bed next mama on the couch
10. made it to the bathroom but never made it out of house

11. big cuz jump up said it's something she need to check

12. for the next move she always get love and respect

13. when you're beginnings like this you don't fear your end

14. and in the middle you just make sure you dump out

15. they told her not to push cause there's no doctor in the house

16. thanks to God no one knew he had a doctor in the house

17. My mama started pushing but I'm not out yet

18. somebody yelled stop the cord wrapped around his neck

19. this could have ended bad I'm here talking so I guess I laugh

20. my Nurse Jackie just learned this in class my very first miracle and for

so glad

21. unwrap the cord slowly hold it

22. wait for the right precise moment

23. cause if you don't why the pulse is still beating,

24. cut too quick and then I wouldn't be breathing

25. one false move and I'll lose

26. every ounce of my blood then I snooze

27. it's been war since day one all your troops are pitiful

28. I'm nowhere near my Pinnacle hey this is just my interview

L.D.

Ok, this is a great album. So with the first song, was that story real, or did you add anything to it for dramatic flair?

Cronyk

Yes, every line in it were correct. 3821 West Jackson St, Chicago, IL is where I was born. My mother went into labor at home. I have always said that this would make a dope song.

L.D.

So it was an at home birth with no doctor? Everything seems to have turned out fine.

Cronyk

I was blessed. The line, "No one knew he had a doctor in the house," has always been the part that amazed me. My big cousin, Jackie, was in nursing school at that time and just happened to be studying labor and delivery. I had my umbilical cord wrapped around my neck, and she knew what to do.

Now having children of my own, I have a better understanding of how much could go wrong with childbirth.

I remember anytime I would get off track; my dad would tell me this story to let me know that I had a purpose for being here.

L.D.

You have lived in TN a significant portion of your life, yet you speak of your birth city with so much admiration, Why is that?

Cronyk

In the line where I say, "but the heart of the land kept me can be to make it out of there. I've heard New York artist say, "If you can make it in New York, you can make it anywhere." That's pushing through the gritty." I'm speaking of how tough we all know it how I feel about Chicago.

The Product

1. You say you got it bad well I got it to

2. No I'm not downing yours I'm simply joining you

3. you got a roof over your head and a pot to piss

4. somebody got it worse than you last night they sleep under a bridge

5. this generation selfish always focused on self

6. how about you take some time to think about somebody else

7. that's what I'm going to do with this song and try to make a difference

8. instead of speaking about my pain I'm going to tell you about the homie Jimmy

9. look he was 18 that's where the story start

10. graduated and made it without catching a charge

11. one day he walkin to the store and seen some flashing lights

12. he probably would have turned back if he knew it's finna changes life

13. cop asked him what you doing on the wrong side of the track

14. he said I live down the map hey this is where I'm zoned at

15. Then turned him around patted him down next on cuffs he slapped

16. said I know you clean but I'm a charge you with this Pack

Chorus— when you're just a product of where you come from/ you will surely end up in trouble/ don't get mad get on your hustle/ and don't be scared to struggle afraid struggle

1. 8 months in a sell feel like he came

breathe

2. talk to his lawyer said I thought we go to court three

3. he fell down on his knees and prayed to GOD

4. jumped up to his feet tell the da I'm going to take the plea

5. In his mind yea he think he free want to see his girl for she have they seed

6. talk to his p.o and try to get a j.o.b

7. but ain't nobody hiring when you got felonies

8. not burger King not Dairy Queen not Taco Bell Nor Mickey D's

9. so what are you supposed to do when your girl needs shoes and a child needs socks

10. go cry the Blues or ask to dealer for his back stock.

11. how long does it take when you

Oppress and kill a man's pride

12. before you take to cups of forget it and gone unleash that beast inside

13. you can try to hate it debate it or tear it apart

14. but you won't understand until you see your family starve

15. Jimmy path was chosen for him he did his part fam

16. but that's what you get for being broke in this Rich land

Chorus— when you're just a product of where you come from/ you will surely end up in trouble/ don't get mad get on your hustle/ and don't be scared to struggle afraid struggle

L. D.

This story is so harsh. How could that happen?

Cronyk

Our society lives in a world of microwave thinkers that will quickly ask, what is the fastest way to feel better? The problem is, you can feel better without being better. Water can be cure headaches in some cases, but most run to pills never even trying to figure out what is causing the pain.

This approach is an epidemic in itself. The first thing that is said when someone from lower income is killed or arrested is, these people put themselves in that situation. I know from first hand this is not always true.

In verse one, I end it with, "cop turned him around, patted him down, next on cuffs he slapped said I know you clean but I'm going charge you with this pack."

We had a story break and hit the news recently about some cops in Alabama. They are under investigation for planting evidence on inner city minorities for the last ten years.

The story I'm speaking of in this song happened in TN. That's two different states, so just think of all the states that get away with such wrong doings.

L. D.

Would you say the jail sentences for a second or third strike are too harsh, especially if the first strike came from a lie?

Cronyk

Yes, they are too harsh. You are giving someone a tougher punishment on the person's FIRST time around.

Now let me be the first to say, I am big on personal responsibility and most of the people you talk to will say the same. None of you see that the actions always complained about are just a symptom and not the cause.

I'll ask. If I placed you in a room full of candy as a child, and said, "Eat all you want. You are not responsible until you are of adulthood," Would you do it? Of course, right now the answer is no, but for those being honest, there isn't a child in the world that would turn it down. Let's replace the candy store with low-income housing, and replace the belly ache with responsibilities of life.

I hear this saying a lot, if I were in that situation, I would do better, and I believe you. Now, what if you are put into that position without the knowledge you have now and no immediate consequences to suffer? Would you come out the same, or would you find your way to the position you are in now? The actions that the system has taken are the cause of the symptoms we see.

L.D.

So does that mean you think we should blame everything on the system?

Cronyk

Not at all, being responsible is part of the solution that needs to happen, but to every action, there is an opposite or equal reaction.

The system creates victims when they infringe upon freedoms. The first casualties are the innocent inmates. Once the innocent ones are released back into a society that doesn't truly believe in a second chance, ("but ain't nobody hiring when you got felonies, not Burger King, not Dairy Queen, not taco bell, nor Mickey D's"),they are not able to find jobs to keep a roof over their heads.

The children are also victims in this situation. Time in prison causes a strain on the relationship between the parent and child. You have kids that grow up feeling as if they are the reason of this situation. They have feelings of resentment. Sometimes this causes a lack of respect for their parent. Depending on how long the parent is away, it may cause their relationship never to be as it should.

The Third victim is the single parent. The system uses this device to help create single parent homes in our society.

The US government had recently put out statics that shows before government assistance, over 81% of low-income households had both parents. As for the other 19 percent, you had the community stepping up to help out where the single parents lacked. And now that number is under 60%. Communities no longer support one another the way they once did. That shows that not only was there little to no problems with single parenting before they stepped in, but government assistance has broken down the foundation our communities once stood on.

They will dare to tell you that at the same time the marches for freedom were going on, blacks were committing crimes against each other. OK, how about we use common knowledge to solve this.

If they had film footage and hardcore evidence to show these marches, why do we not have the same for all of these so-called crimes? I'm not now, nor will I ever be OK with where the inner city is at this point. What I do know is: if I want to make any changes to wake my people up, I must first treat the cause and not the symptoms.

Trust Issues

1. I see the media they'll flip in a second (Flip Flip)
2. I know I jumped right in with no introduction but I don't think it's necessary
3. cause everybody they got opinions from the couch they'll never ever know the truth
4. cause when you try to show these folks the truth they don't want to focus on the truth
5. I got a question what happened to the g code it
6. seems like we all want to win so we livin by the cheat code
7. I'm riding around on my solo flipping game on my dolo
8. cause most of the dudes no all of this dudes are down to talk to the popos so

Chorus- I can't trust these people can't

trust these people no /I can't I don't want to/ I can't trust these people can't trust these people no/ I can't I don't want to/ look how they come round look how they come round/ they waving they guns round /they ready to dump out somebody got shot down /look how they come round look how they come round/ they pulling they guns out they ready to dumb out

1. Lil Tony he was sitting on the Block somebody rolled threw he got hit
2. before the news heard what happened they done already said it's bout a brick
3. one of the dudes in the car got caught swearing that he'll never snitch
4. but we done all seen First 48 they start crying and then they go ahead and flip

5. it's a trip the whole cycle really done turn

6. Crack dropped in the 80's 35 years later and we still ain't learn

7. nobody gains from watching when I say it's hot it's going burn

8. but instead of listening to my words they still want to take you turn

9. I got a question what happened to the g code

10. it seems like we all want to win so we living by the cheat code

11. riding around in my solo flipping game with my dolo

12. cause most of these dudes no all of these dudes down to talk to the popo so

Chorus— I can't trust these people can't trust these people no /I can't I don't want to/ I can't trust these people can't trust these people no/ I can't I don't

want to/ look how they come round
look how they come round/ waving
their guns round there pulling their
guns out somebody got shot down /look
how they come around look how they
come round /they pulling them guns
out /they ready to dumb out they
waving them guns round
1. raw intent is how they convict are
you really open up listening
2. cause I'm goin speak yea I'm goin
teach best believe that they listen In
3. the biggest thing that they fear is
somebody at the bottom with a brain
4. that can dodge they whips and
break they chains and then started
winning at the game
5. focused on better but don't think
like the masses
6. walking in church seeing the Fraud
and then questions they're asking

7. looking for air and you're gasping cause this matrix's world is so plastic
8. the Have Nots Just Gotta Have It so we stretch the truth just like elastic
9. I got a question what happened to the G-Code
10. it seems like we all want to win so we living by the cheat code
11. riding around on my solo flipping game on my dolo
12. cause most of these dudes no all of these dudes down to talk to the popos so

L.D.

OK, it sounds like you are leaving no stone unturned. So explain this to me, do you not trust the system or the people?

Cronyk

I don't trust anyone, but I created this song to speak about the media, all forms of media. Perception is everything. You honestly have not grown as a person until you can perceive a situation from another person's perspective. The scary thing about this is someone can quickly alter your perception if they know how.

"I see the media they'll flip in a second" A drug bust goes on. After a news station gathers bits of information, they come in with breaking news like, "We are here at the corner of blank where the cops just found four guns, $20,000 in cash, and 100 pounds of marijuana." They'll start using adjectives and statements such as the drug dealer, thugs, or have ties to gangs.

Now take that same situation the same amount of illegal guns, drugs, and money. But, for some reason this time the person is a son, father, troubled soul caught up in the wrong path. Why did the adjectives change?

L.D.

I don't know; you tell me.

Cronyk

"This matrix world is so plastic. The have-nots just got to have it. So we stretch the truth just like elastic." Because it's a cop, Senator, or someone they feel it's important not to demonize.

Before making sure they have the right story, they will spew out assumptions or hearsay. The information is typically incorrect.

Have you ever watched a major news station after a tragedy strikes? They will begin with one dramatic story that is thrown way out of proportion, and by the end of the day have an entirely different spin on what truly happened. By the time the truth comes out, people have judged the situation on all of the opinions and incorrect information that the media gav in the beginning.

They grab for the information that will give them more Television ratings.

It has gone from informative to entertainment. People are looking for the Reality TV wow effect, so they attempt to give it to the public, even at others expense.

They never apologize for getting information incorrect. They allow peoples' names to be drug through the mud, by running a story over and over.

Now, when the person is found not guilty of all charges they'll say it once during the day and leave it alone. No one is home watching the news at 3 pm everyone is in school or at work. So, to millions of viewers, you are still guilty.

Every Time

Chorus- Every time I watch the news
it leaves me so confused /every every
every/ every time I watch the news it
leaves me so confused/ confused

1. Every time I watch the news it
leaves me so confused

2. you keep praying for that day I just
see my people lose

3. we never did nothing to you but I
could see that hatred ooze

4. out your pores for me boy you can't
wait to see me snooze

5. just like them crooked coppas
grabbing choppas trying to kill my
brother

6. for your chest you need a vest just
like Jimmy need a rubber

7. for protection todays a Blessing by
the end you learned a lesson

8. How it feel to have a Target on you
just cause you parked a Lexus

9. television for the souls have no love
gunned down in Cold Blood
10. besides your pic they title Thug
11. is tha caption when it happens
there's no action but the people call it
tragic
12. On the stand they got the captain
when he leave I bet he laughing
Chorus- every time I watch the news it
leaves me so confused /every every
every/ every time I watch the news it
leaves me so confused confused /every
time I watch the news and leave me so
confused/ every every /every time I
watch the news it leave me so confused
confused
1. Every time I watch the news it
leaves me so confused
2. you keep praying for the day I just
see my people lose
3. he standing in the club with a dub

like he won

4. his homie bout to show up pulling out a pocket full of ones

5. pills and dank pollute our brain why da liquor numbs our soul

6. now your squad is about to box or let it pop over a camel toe

7. almost killed a man what saved his life is the hammer Froze

8. it's like the whole Hood got a sickness and I'm searching for antidote

9. ask me if I think I'm better and I answer hell know

10. I've been in that orange suit when they close the sell do

11. look we in the same Creek and neither got a sailboat

12. how could I judge you I used to sell dope

Chorus- every time I watch the news it leaves me so confused/ every every/

every time I watch the news it leaves
me so confused confused /every time I
watch the news it leaves me so
confused /every time I watch the news
and leaves me so confused confused

L.D.

Now we have other characters added to the conversation.
Sticking with the media first, for what do we hold them
responsible?

Cronyk

"Gunned down in cold blood, beside your pic they title thug."
We hold them responsible for causing confusion and fear
among everyday people.

L.D.

Is there a way to change it?

Cronyk

I learned something very imperative in the last few years.

Bill Cosby was attacked. I'm not arguing a point, just would
like to emphasize something. He made sure to file a lawsuit
for feeling his name was slandered.

In the movie, Straight Out of Compton, as soon as Jerry
Heller heard the dis by Ice Cube, he said, "I'll sue." May I ask
who is willing to look at the situation of Blacks in America
and file a grievance?

We have all been classified as the group of people you pull
over with extreme caution. We are dismantled in every area of
the media, and we are spoken of like our complaints are urban
legends.

We should legally fight back. I've heard the only way to make
a business change its ways is to touch their profits.

L.D.

How can the people make changes to this situation?

Cronyk

"When it happens, there's no action, but the people call it tragic" Stop marching for no reason. Why are we holding signs, blocking interstates, and confronting police officers? Do we not understand they just uphold the law?

L.D.

So, you don't think we should protest?

Cronyk

I believe we are only doing the part that has been shown to us in the media. Every year in February, you are programmed with pictures of freedom riders, but they never show the rest of the story. They had laws put into play. They had a dialogue with senators, governors, mayors, and the people that could truly help change the situation.

Our young people are only speaking to the media. You can show videos all day long. You can make personal blogs and get a million likes on social media sites. That is not going to pass any laws. For things to change, you have to get laws passed. The police only uphold the laws set in place.

We all have felt that cops get away with things. When in reality they beat cases because of legislation that protects their actions.

Instead of only protesting, we need to write out what we want, and make a plan.

If you can get enough signatures on a petition, they have to start listening. We should be having a conversation with them about the needs and wants of our communities. Let's make our walks a means to an end, that's all I'm saying.

Hello Officer

Chorus- How am I supposed to feel/
when the one that's supposed to protect
us is trying to kill me /how am I
supposed to feel /when the one's we
paid to protect us is trying to kill we
/hello officer hello officer hello
officer hello officer how am I really
supposed to feel about it /hello officer
hello officer hello officer hello officer
at least you could be real about it/

1. what up chief how you doing
Lieutenant
2. I know you ready to lock me up
because that's just part of your
business
3. but you don't like me and you don't
even know me I'm just keeping it real
stating the fact
4. I was born with two strikes whats
that I. liked my hair and I'm a rock
my tatts.

5. Plus the jail house has been compromised it's opened up to the market

6. so anybody or everybody can go and try to make a quick profit

7. I ain't the smartest man in the world but I'm good at logic

8. when it comes to making a big Quick buck everybody down with getting it poppin

9. it's been too many put off in a coffin with they face-down and they hands up

10. you took the oath to Serve and Protect so put your gun down and try man up

11. look everybody in the hood ain't wrong and everybody doing bad ain't bad

12. a lot of people out here living life just trying to get more than they done

ever had

13. take the time to live in my shoes
lose it all without crying the blues

14. get locked up and not have no clue
what you did wrong they got no proof

15. I thought it's innocent until you
get proven guilty how I'm supposed to
plead my case if you done kill me

16. now the problem going keep on
building until you stop killing up all
our children

Chorus- how I'm supposed to feel
when the ones you pay to protect us is
trying to kill me /how am I supposed
to feel when the one's supposed to
protect us is trying to kill we /hello
officer hello officer hello officer hello
officer I'm really supposed to feel
about it/ hello officer hello officer
hello officer hello officer at least you
could be real about it

1. bump Jesse Jackson third finger to Al Sharpton

2. we out here living this real life and they just part of the problem

3. Martin Luther got shot right in front of their face his time up

4. instead of going riding hard for their homeboy they just lined up

5. Trayvon got shot yeah and he was black

6. Michael Brown got shot yeah and he was black

7. Justin Taylor got shot yeah and he was white

8. Andy Lopez he got hit up he was Hispanic they don't care about nobody rights

9. said they protected not nobody rights so your heart start pounding when you see the flashing lights

10. media spending like all of the

height without the Blood Sweat and Tears and sacrifice

11. they said Burn It to the Ground so we flamed

12. you took the first second and the third shot so now don't blame us

13. Mike Jackson said it right they don't really care about us

14. so us coming together and getting it right I know they really doubt us

15. I thought it was innocent until we get proven guilty how I'm supposed to plead my case if you done kill me

16. now the problem is going to keep on building until you stop killing up all the children

Chorus- how I'm supposed to feel when the one's we pay to protect us is trying to kill me/ how I'm supposed to feel when the one's that supposed to protect us is trying to kill we/ hello

officer hello officer hello officer hello
officer how I'm really supposed to feel
about it/ hello officer hello officer
hello officer hello officer at least you
could be real about it

L.D.

Oh wow, these two songs back two back. So, I think we can see what your stance is on the issues involving blacks and cops.

Cronyk

Where do you believe, I stand?

L.D.

Well, they are bullies doing whatever they want. They are drunk with power purposely targeting a specific set of people.

Cronyk

I only believe some do that. If you look at these lines, you'll see my view is different from some.

I said, "Trayvon got shot yeah he was black/ Michael Brown got shot yeah he was black/ Dillon Taylor got shot yeah he was white/ Andy Lopez got hit up; he was Hispanic they don't care about nobody's rights."

It is a power issue to me. Also, I feel that it's a part of their training.

L.D.

Do you think there are just a few bad cops?

Cronyk

No, I don't believe that only the officers are wrong. I believe the system is bad. It's all connected, and it's nothing new. Please pay attention to the actions that you see every day.

The system is set up to prosecute differently based on economics. We have already addressed the media has made our culture appear to be a group of super aggressive assassins coming to hunt you down. If they are consistently trained to believe this, that is exactly what they will see. So, it's more than just cops are against us; the system as a whole is.

L.D.

You mentioned that you feel like this situation affects more than just us. Please Explain.

Cronyk:

Raw numbers will answer that. At this point, One Hundred and Thirty blacks have been shot by police officers. However, over 500 people, as a whole, have been killed in police shootings. Yes, this number only includes the deaths that have had grievances filed. We have a grave situation going on, and it is overlooked.

We have confusion going on when we truly need compassion. The way I see it is, if someone I knew and someone you knew got killed on the same day, it is painful for the both of us. Instead of fighting each other, we should be trying to figure out a solution.

L.D.

So, you can support All Lives Matter?

Cronyk

No. I support Black Lives Matter because they are standing up for what we believe in, safety for the children, women, and men of my community. I say and mean this from the bottom of my heart. The same way other cultures have aided in our cause, if they stand up for themselves, I'm willing to stand and support.

L.D.

That makes sense to me you are willing to give them back what they are giving you. This blows my mind; I didn't know that many people were dying at the hands of police. Just to be clear, are you saying you don't think it is racism?

Cronyk

Oh, no racism exists. I just don't see it like everyone else. My view is more of a systematic base of racism. Not saying that I haven't seen it in other ways. The system is the glue that keeps it all going.

While researching for this album, I came across an article that showed just how manipulative the system is. In 2007, Congress had to vote on renewing parts of the Voting Rights Acts of 1965. The Justice Department's spokesman, Eric W. Holland, attempted to spin it by saying, "It's important for folks to know that the right to vote – even if those sections expire – will not expire." When I read his statement, my only question was how can anyone honestly assume we have equal rights, if you have to vote on my rights?

L.D.

The fact that it was only ten years ago makes me cringe. Our generation has broken a lot of the barriers but obviously not enough.

Cronyk

Oh, believe me, it gets worse. I recently read an article written by Ryan Gabrielson and Topher Sanders titled, "How a $2

Roadside Drug Test Sends Innocent People to Jail". It reads; Widespread evidence shows that these tests routinely produce false positives. Why are departments and prosecutors across the country still using them?

"The jailhouse has been compromised; it's opened up to the market." The profits of a modern slave trade are of more importance to massa.

L.D.

So, you think prison is slavery?

Cronyk

Of course, I believe it is slavery, for more than one reason. The story they tell us is blacks came over during the slave trade. They were treated like property lower than cattle but higher than women. When in fact it was, the cheapest workforce they could find. Now, who occupies most of those jail cells owned by these companies? Once again, they have free labor, and all they had to do is work with the system they helped create.

L.D.

At this point of the album, you decided to switch the tone, why?

Cronyk

You can only take in so much at one time. Plus the topic, I turned to deserves as much attention as the first. I believe if we can get this one thing right, we have a chance of correcting our course.

L.D.

So, what are you trying to teach in this part of the Album?

Cronyk

Relaying a Foundation, any kingdom that can be destroyed can be rebuilt. The only thing needed for this to happen is an inspiration. Money, power, nor religion can motivate a man like the love he has for the woman that captures his heart…

Paradise

Chorus- You're my supercalifragilistic Expialidocious baby / take my hand I'll take you away to my Paradise my a baby (repeat twice)

1. excuse me can I have a second of your time

2. cause there's a land you lost and I want to help you find

3. First let me put down this notebook and run through all these lines

4. You've heard your beautiful you super thick and you're so so fine

5. well I resign from using lines that you heard from another

6. want to see you sitting close not searching for a Distant Lover

7. not going act like you already know tell me what makes you different

8. remembering every line because this man knows how to listen

9. I know you got a million that would love to hold your hand

10. keep telling you that they really don't want you but keep watching the back of your pants

11. showing you what they could buy mixed with lies and a perfect plan

12. trying to be the bud to get that butterfly to land

13. Hey your last dude said he smart and he had a thought

14. to leave you and he ended up with a thot

15. said you was nothing hey said you was nothing

16. but I like the way you turn nothing into something Your my

Chorus- supercalifragilistic Expialidocious baby /take my hand I'll take you away to my Paradise my lady (repeat twice)

1. what took you so long could it be you thinking about us

2. Yea you can deal with the buster's but me myself I'm too much

3. did you like the vocab I got a knack for words

4. so I could tell you a million things you never heard

5. Oh how I'm doing alright still cool Just Chillin grillin plotting out a way for me to make a million

6. ~~I'm a second I'm finna hit the ride and go~~ in a sec I'm finna hit the

7. ~~The passenger sit empty come and occupy it fo~~ ride and go

8. the passenger seat empty come and occupy it for

9. we'll picture this somebody wanted to Grant every wish

10. that constantly give good convo

and plenty mental gifts

11. when you down a single phone call could give a mental lift

12. remembering every day nothing is ever missed

13. hey your last dude said he's smart so he had a thought

14. to leave you and he ended up with a thot

15. said you was nothing hey said you was nothing

16. but I like the way you turned nothing into something your my

Chorus-
supercalifragilisticexpialidocious baby /take my hand I'll take you away to my Paradise my lady (repeat twice)

1. was different about me is most dudes want to think they a pimp

2. when they come to having women

they need 4 5 and 6
3. me I just need one for her I'll get all
the gifts
4. and for me she do all of her tricks
5. baby I aim too please I'm a bull's-
eye hitta Go Getta
6. if you lost in the foreign land I'm a
Go Getta
7. if she ride for me I'm down for her
I'm a go with her
8. you will never worry about these
lames I'm a Go Reala
9. your last dude said he's smart and
he had a thought
10. to leave you and he ended up
with a thot
11. said you was nothing hey said you
was nothing
12. but I like the way you turn
nothing into something your my
Chorus- supercalifragilistic

Expialidocious baby/ take my hand
I'll take you away to a paradise my
lady (repeat twice)

L.D.

Paradise, what is this song about?

Cronyk

Self-respect, the way you treat yourself is important. The people that you hang around are often a reflection of yourself. If you can describe your partner as promiscuous, what does that say about you?

With songs depicting women as being alright with being with multiple partners, called anything other than their given name, or down for anything, people have been lead to believe that women are ok with being disrespected and that is a lie.

People are pressured into suppressing what they actually feel is appropriate for attention from the opposite sex. This means that they are sometimes willing to put all morals and values on the back burner.

There are some that love the bad boy. They find themselves jumping from relationship to relationship with guys that have no intention of treating them the way they deserve to be treated. So instead of taking the time to learn to love their self-first or choosing a person to help build a kingdom, they constantly play games.

They have bought into the Roman Greek philosophy of sleep with as many as you can until you settle.

L.D.

I noticed that this song had no sexual implications. Why?

Cronyk.

It's crazy that we live in a day in time that this is a question that is asked. Everything seems to be geared towards sex. That seems to be one of the main ideas in people's minds. You can't give a compliment nor do an act of kindness without someone automatically assuming you are thirsty or desperate.

The song is just saying hello, that's it. "Excuse me may I have a second of your time" is not a pickup line; it's a respectful greeting for men and women.

I don't want to be around anyone that would allow me to disrespect them.

L.D.

I've never heard a guy say that. I can bet you have a great reason behind it so enlighten me.

Cronyk

A relationship between the opposite sexes should be more than just a physical attraction. I tell my sons and my daughters the same thing. Honestly, I feel that both young men and young women should stay whole until marriage. I'm shocked neither one of them has asked me why didn't I wait until marriage.

L.D

What would your response be to that question?

Cronyk

I am prepared to tell them I recently woke up from the slave state of mind, and a lot of our community still has this mentality. It is critical to find the right person before deciding to make that commitment. Having sex a person is making a covenant with them.

L.D

How is this, a slave state of mind?

Cronyk

The women in our community are willing to put this government into their family issues. They are running to "massa" because it has been instilled in them to do so. Our men have children with women without intentions of making a family. What I mean is they're running around solely breeding to make more workers for the plantation.

L.D.

I hope this song is a hit and the message quickly spreads.

Breakfast

1. ever had breakfast with candle lights
2. well shut the blinds cut off the lights
3. yep had a wonderful night
4. and with everything you did I know you worked up an appetite
5. so come over here but sit right there
6. this is your moment I got it babe I don't need no help
7. everything is ready for you all of my meats are prepped
8. what you don't see this apron girl I'm your top shelf
9. I can cook it baby whatever you're into
10. the food to feed your soul and open your mental
11. Yea that's my sharp knife I call it my Ginsu
12. Now all I need from you is to pick

out the menu

Bridge- if you really want it if you really want it / all you gotta do is say it and I will get right on it / yea you perform when you was on it now before you get too yawning/ just tell me what we're eating in the morning

Chorus- I said I want to make love to you/ I don't want to rush I want to feel your touch/ I said I want to make love to you /I don't want to rush I want to feel you touch/ this is for Lovers Only /so turn off the lights and we can get it right /this is for Lovers Only /so turn off the lights and let's get it right

1. how you feel about what we do

2. I want to cook the food that'll gets you in the mood

3. walking in the dark well come give me your clue

4. cause the right dish at war time

we'll call it a truce

5. here go your appetizer simply some diced fruit

6. Avocados and peaches strawberries pineapples too

7. I want to be your waiter and you're my only table

8. so what's your order to fulfill I know that I'm able

Bridge- if you really want it if you really want it /all you gotta do is say it and I will get right on it /you performed when you was on it /now before you get to yawning/ just tell me what we eating in the morning

Chorus- I said I want to make love to you/ I don't want to rush I want to feel your touch / I said I want to make love to you I don't want to rush I want to feel your touch/ this is for Lovers Only /so turn off the lights and

we can get it right / this is for Lovers
Only / so turn off the lights and we
can get it right

1. how you like your eggs scrambled
with cheese
2. Oh I do that with ease
3. so you want an omelet
4. I like to flip you on your stomach
5. how you like your grits
6. runny or thick oh like you that's
super cute
7. I hope you know you really got me
pleased
8. and I'm so so Southern in my castle
girl you gotta eat

Chorus— I said I want to make love to
you/ I don't want to rush I want to feel
your touch/ I said I want to make love
to you/ I don't want to rush I want to
feel your touch/ this is for Lovers
Only/

so turn off the lights and we can get it right /this is for Lovers Only/ so turn off the lights and we can get it right

Cronyk

Keeping the focus on relationships, I was trying to get guys to do more, just the overall push for men to be men and to aim to please their woman. Sometimes we forget all of the sweet gestures we were doing to win their hearts. Once we win our queen's favor, we sometimes become comfortable. If not reminded, it's easy to slip into this state of being comfortable. So, the song was just a reminder not to be so relaxed all of the time. Make every moment, every second special, because she's special to you.

L.D.

I think that is great advice. I love it. My favorite line was: "I want to be your waiter, and you're my only table."

Cronyk

When I sat down to write this song, the concept was the guy that loves his woman. I'm as blunt as possible; there's no way you can listen to or play the type of music that disrespects women and say you love your spouse. It just doesn't go together. Calling her out of her name and telling her she is nothing does not equal love.

And tell me why you would listen to those songs while your daughters, nieces, or any young girls are around. You're teaching with your actions that you, someone they love and trust, is alright with the derogatory songs. When they get older and date someone, you're making it alright for them to be called all these words or get treated this way.

L.D.

I've said the same thing forever. I don't listen to, nor support any music that does. No matter whom the artist is that sings it.

Cronyk

I wish you would teach that to more women. Chris Rock described it best he said; They will be dancing to a song and telling you he's not talking about me. I know women that would snap your neck if you called them out of their name. These songs somehow find their way on our culture's radios.

L.D.

Now I have to say it. In the last song no sex, but in this one you were very creative with your words.

Cronyk

Yes, I was aiming for that old school feel, where the grownups knew what was going on, and the children had no clue. We have to put the line back up to recreate the standards our parents set.

So I chose to use food as a metaphor. This song is about satisfying your partner. When you eat a healthy meal, it makes you happy. Real cooks enjoy watching others enjoy their dishes.

Stretched Greys

1. Since you have asked a question this is how I choose to reply

2. cause in my song you know that I could never tell a lie

3. you've been fine ever since the first time

4. that I looked into your eyes and I ever said hi

5. next i need to know your mind that took us no time

6. I emptied out my pockets you a quarter so I threw away the dimes

7. I like the way you handle your biz the way you take care of the kids

8. and make sure that I'm straight before I ever leave the crib

9. then she told me you don't want to see me touch a pack

10. this is ours you got my back and you going to pick up where I Slack

11. hey the house the cars the jewels and the clothes they can get it back
12. ever try to come and touch you then they head I crack
13. so many waiting on our downfall
14. but we going to stand tall rain sleet snow and all
15. you're my fine wine that I have been sipping on at dinner time
16. so that should let you know that we get better with time

Chorus- I'm a love your gray hair gray hair and your stretch marks/ said I'm gone love your gray hair gray hair and your stretch marks/ cause we get better with time/ I'm a love your gray hair gray hair and your stretch marks/ said I'm going to love your gray hair gray and stretch marks/ cause we get better with time

1. satin sheets I require most people call me sire

2. I'm a king come be Queen to this Empire

3. your wants your needs I want to fulfill

4. whenever you're the Damsel in Distress I want to be Your Man of Steel

5. so chill with me baby for a minute ain't no contest

6. 11 years later want tell my maker you're my conquests

7. different from a trap Queen wanting longevity

8. instead of letting me chass the bread you keep pulling out the Best in Me

9. Love conversating with you just a raise your mental

10. making love in the morning just to please your physical

11. listen to every song making sure that I'm lyrical

12. read with you pray with you just to raise your spiritual

13. so many waiting on a downfall

14. but we going to stand tall rain sleet snow and all

15. you're my fine wine I've been sipping on at dinner time

16. so that should let you know that we get better with time

Chorus- I'm a love your gray hair gray hair and your stretch marks/ said I'm a love your gray hair gray hair and your stretch marks/ cause we get better with time/ I'm a love your gray hair gray hair and your stretch marks/ said I'm a love your gray hair gray

hair and your stretch marks cause we
get better with time

L.D.

I love it! Your rap song is one I've not heard in a while that focuses on growing old together. It has the Method Man Mary J feel. What inspired this one?

Cronyk

Age, I had to mature enough to be able to write this song. Longevity has become a memory, and its enemy is self-gratification. It is not about "US" anymore. It's about "ME." I know a lot of old couples that have stood the test of time. Their primary focus was not what or how can I benefit from this? It was about the bigger picture. They were truly a team.

L.D.

Do you think forever is still possible, or are the times to different know?

Cronyk

Let's look at the time, and list all of the distractions. Our generation's number 1 reason for divorce is money. That's why I made sure to put it up front:

"The house, the car, the jewels, and the clothes they can get it back/ but if they ever touch you then they head I crack."

We have twice the opportunities our great-grandparents had, but we are letting money split us up. The love of money is the root of all evil. It's okay to have material things, but you shouldn't love them more than the people that are supposed to matter to you.

Number two is obvious, and I understand it, infidelity. I think that we don't hold the same values on this because our moral compass is off. Sleeping around with each other is glorified now.

It is alright to step out on someone is you are not happy with the way things are going. Being a side chick is normal. It is a goal of a lot of young people. We have people that feel as if as long as you are going home to one person, it doesn't matter what you are doing while outside of the home, not thinking of the long-term damage it can do to a person that you may love.

L.D.

I can agree that there are a lot of females feel that being the side chick is alright now. There are some that have taken over the actions of guys. How did we get off?

Cronyk

We once looked at our women with great pride and admiration; that has changed. Our women understood the unseen battles men fought for them and had respect for them. Like everything else, this too has changed. The battle of the sexists has split us up. So we end up back at the word respect. If you don't respect the men and women you come from, you're not respecting yourself.

L.D.

So not only the stretch greys of your spouse but the stretch greys of your mom as well.

Cronyk

You've heard the saying is if you want to know how a man will treat you. Look at how he treats his mom. I use it both ways the way she respects her dad will tell you a lot.

L.D.

So what is number three?

Cronyk

The third is probably to me the most important communication. A simple talk through situations could solve a lot of problems. I'm sure none of these problems are new, but everyone would like to think that they're different. You want to be happy, and you're not. Is it somebodies' fault right? Nope, it's all yours.

While speaking with my grandma one day, she said something very profound. She told me to pick a topic and think of how I felt about it at the ages of 10, 18, and 28 years old. You should try it. What you will discover is, no matter what the subject is, your feelings about it changed with your age. Your feelings changed because you mature as you become older.

L.D.

That is so true, but how does that help you to build this foundation?

Cronyk

"Love conversating with you just to raise your mental."

Conversation is a vital key, because of your growth and change. Therefore, the conversation is needed to inform your spouse of where you are in your growth, keeping you both tied together mentally.

"Making love in the morning just to please your physical."

The body follows the mind. If the communication is good, this becomes natural.

"Listen to every song making sure that I'm lyrical."

I customized this for me, but take an interest in what your spouse does. Don't make every talk about you.

"Read with you, pray with you just to raise your spiritual."

When you come together as one and activate mind, body, and soul forever is very possible.

Cronyk

How could you say you love me but not take the time to speak to me?

How can I learn if you don't teach?

At what point did you decide it was ok for the generations after you to go back into bondage?

May I know who forgot to remind me that I came from a great nation?

How can I stand if you don't believe in me?

Did you know that the information you thought not to teach me would be the weapon our enemies used to attack me?

As you read the next set of songs, keep these questions in mind.

Oshea

man the streets ain't for err body my hitta- totting heats ain't for err body my hitta- graveyards ain't for the scared bodies my killa- but the graveyards for them dead bodies my killa- you ain't been on the block you ain't stack figures I was posted on the block with the rock hitta- talking bout the streets Oshea got a lot in him doing dirt man forget it put some shots in him- got to feed my fam so I'm out here working I swear I star going hard when Nate got shot- start selling got money thought he start twerking got low cause I heard Ray got locked- man you know I can't go like that people ask why I roll like that- cause they try to take mine and we load up the tommy slide through and we blow right back

Lil D

I know hittas in the pen they ain't done yet I know killas in the dirt boy they done wet/ say he want to be a thug he don't want to be a thug when he feeling them slugs to his stomach/ dropped out of school for that money/ he ain't making no money boy he you a dummy/ I'm just saying the streets gone get ugly go stay on the block and get bloody/ on 19 looking like he 30/ swear them drugs got him looking real dirty/ the consequences of this lifestyle hitta/ you ain't ready for this lifestyle hitta turn around my hitta/ can't nobody save you when the lights down/ one shot headshot now you lifed out/ police don't care so it's lights out/ no case no face how you feel now

Chorus– I swear that you noisy/ but I heard what you spoken / it's two in the morning I'm not doing wrong/ I'm not coming home you blowing my zone/ why can't you leave me alone

1. I know that you think I play about what I say

2. and know that you think that I play around but I don't play

3. you thinking you smooth boy thinking you cute boy

4. girls talking to you cuz your bread no clue boy

5. on the Block every day trying to get loot boy

6. the homie that be riding with you he be the shoot boy

7. but you better go to school boy ain't telling you be a lame and try to be a Schoolboy

8. but you better go to school but before you end up in the pen and you acting like a do boy

9. make up your bed pick up your cup

10. if you don't eat now then you don't get enough and that ain't real and it show ain't what's up

11. so pay attention because the pen don't play

12. they'll find you somewhere DOA

13. trapped in a Cell you can get away

14. it's six of them you ain't got a gun but they got to Shank

15. I'm just trying to tell you youngin what go on in there if you ain't down with it set you won't live long in there

16. they going to try to tell you to set up a home in there too many people

died for Freedom you don't belong in
there
Chorus- I swear that you noisy/ but I
heard what you spoken / it's two in
the morning I'm not doing wrong/ I'm
not coming home you blowing my
zone/ why can't you leave me alone

Don Dadda

This is yo life this is yo moment
this is the time you make yo decision to see if you want it
Cause if you want it then you got to go get it
but don't be bullshitting this life that you living is about
choices you make
and what you put in it
you wanna live right or you wanna live wrong
wanna be smart wanna get your hustle on
wanna be cool wanna be hard
pull chicken heads on the boulevard
or you wanna go to school and get ya education
when you try to make it is when they start haten
situations you face with every damn day will have you
feeling like I really can't take it
got to keep going got to keep moving got a good brain you
just need to learn to use it
keep your friends close and your enemies closer you can
do drugs but just don't abuse them
and keep your composer over situation you in
and keep one thing in mind it's family until the end

Chorus- I swear that you noisy/ but I heard what you spoken / it's two in the morning I'm not doing wrong/ I'm not coming home you blowing my zone/ why can't you leave me alone

L.D.

Who are the guests on this song?

Cronyk

My family, Don Dadda Da Gr8, Lil D, and Oshea.

L.D.

This one I need a breakdown on. It doesn't sound like the rest of the album.

Cronyk

The breakdown is simple. You have two different generations on one song. I feel that open communication and realistic dialogue with the generation behind each of us is very important.

Somewhere along the line, we've gotten caught up with having to work, wanting to have fun, catching up with old friends, etc. We're not doing much to teach or encourage the future generation we helped create.

I wanted to reach out to the younger generation, and wake up the older generation. Somewhere along the line, we all have dropped the ball.

L.D.

So Don, Do you agree on the conversation lacking in your eyes?

Don Dadda Da Gr8

I'd agree. Take my verse. It's just a conversation between my son who just turned 18 and me. It's like an introduction to manhood.

L.D.

So you feel it's the elder's fault for the actions of the youth?

Cronyk

I feel that this was a planned attack as far as separating the older generation from the younger generation. The easiest way to destroy a platoon is by cutting off communication with its leaders.

They killed all of the positive leaders. Then at the same time gave handouts and high positions to the women. They kicked out the men.

Not trying to take up for the actions of this wild crazy generation that we are witnessing, but I will be honest they haven't had adequate guidance. They cannot teach themselves. If we don't talk to this generation, how are we to expect these young people to know or understand when they're out of line?

I meant what I said in my bars "you better to go to school boy, I ain't telling you to be a lame and try to be a school boy. But you better go to school boy before you end up in the pin and you are acting like a do boy." This reality is not often shared with our youth properly. Most songs talk about incarceration like it is ok, helping the revolving door stay in the rotation.

L.D.

Dropping knowledge!

Cronyk

From the beginning of time, every culture passed on its knowledge through conversations. Before they had a written language, everything was verbal. Someone sat down to tell stories to the children. This way, they knew what was important to do and how to bring joy and honor to their culture.

So when I look at the youth, I see a generation of young men that have no fear. The youth are willing and ready to tear up a city because they feel people are treating them unjustly, or they're coming to the aid of a helpless elder. I don't see a band of thugs, and I don't see a gang of hoodlums. I'm looking at a platoon that has no guidance and a lack of leadership.

L.D.

I like how you put together your song. Cronyk you are focusing on the leadership they need, while Don is giving a rite of passage message to the young men.

Don Dadda Da Gr8

Yea, stating the fact that this is YOUR life and YOUR time to choose what you want to do in life. Anything is possible, but it's going to be a struggle regardless what you do. When you decide to live right, there are going to be way more obstacles to endure and fight through, but keep your faith, and you can get through anything that life throws your way yaadaaamtalmbout.

L.D.

I honestly do.

This that track

1. Dude you don't want to see in a dark alley if we got a problem we can go handle it

2. flows been damaging I'm a dismantle them you don't really want to stand nowhere near where the mantle is

3. (let's go) I'm tired of playing nice in this life or just Faking It

4. (let's go) since I'm done with games I'm strapped up and I'm taking it

5. (let's go) the bar you set for the music Biz I'm breaking it

6. (let's go) your world is small and been rollin smooth but I'm quaking it

7. you don't really want it got a hundred grand on it go to war with your squad pimpin I'm a stand on it

8. hardest goon in the room you ain't got a chance homie your platoon take a stand I'm a put my man on it

9. Ridin dirty with the 9 and you know my hand on it fly high in the sky ground I'm a land on it

10. trying to kill my whole community yea you planned on it I got an army right beside me and they won't stand for it

11. in war what would you play with me for murking you before you ever get to the door

12. I soar yep I'm hang on em but first I'm a bang on em cause master done loosen the chain on em

13. infer red so clear I spit wit a aim on em poppin ice cold sickles so I won't leave a stain on em

14. been cronyk for years I ain't gone change on em you a fraud claiming real just change yo lane homie

,15. For real I cut the cake to make a wish my whole team getting a bank

16. can't make mistake the stakes is high so get your hand off my plate
17. for real spit positive energy I know the whole world want to get at me
18. I'm a king do you know what that mean so I only bow down to the one that delivered me Chorus-this that I will never fall behind track this that I'm a education they mind track this that I'm forever on my grind track they say they this well I guess I'm that
1. dude you don't want to see in a dark alley if we got a problem we can go handle it
2. flows been damaging I'm a dismantle them you don't really want to stand nowhere near where the mantle is
3. they say you a youngin this is OG medicine taught by veteran

4. they say I'm to lovin when I'm the gatekeeper Lames I won't let em in

5. they say they be Thuggin the way you walk around in life your only true evidence

6. so they shouldn't play you for nothing cause what I got planned mentally they never heard of it

7. so I'm trying to calm myself before I bomb myself

8. should I numb myself before I snap dumb out here

9. too late for fakes I see the yard full of snakes

10. got the antidote for Venom so like beef you get ate

11. humble meek with my steak but a feast on my plate

12. got a problem with me pimp we could meet face-to-face

13. good morning woke up and I'm scorching talk to Lady tortoise told me to go torch em did it

14. you gone need an inhaler saw industry failure

15. so I'm coming to nail you get it
Chorus- this that I will never fall behind Track this that I'm Forever on my grind track this that I'm a educate they mind track they say they this well I guess I'm That

L.D.

You sound as if you are ready for war on this one. Towards who is the aggression aimed?

Cronyk

"Dude you don't want to see in a dark alley if you got a problem we can go handle it." For me, this line is a self-check. It is a reminder that I can't stand when people turn positive and get soft. In war, if your troops feel you have lost your edge, they stop wanting to follow your orders.

L.D.

You're speaking of that unguided platoon in the last conversation.

Cronyk

Yes, why should they listen? The only advice they are receiving is to stand down and watch others trample their God-given rights. This generation has sat in classes with instructors that have taught them of all civil liberties promised.

L.D.

So what are you saying to them?

Cronyk

"Tried to kill my whole community yea you planned on it. Got an army right beside me and they won't stand for it." I am saying that I'm willing to get in line and play my part. From researching to find our actual history, to coming up with real solutions to the problems we face.

L.D.

Would you say this is the doing of the industry or the artist?

Cronyk

"They say you too loving when I'm the gatekeeper lames I won't let 'em in." The children in the industry get a pass because they are not old enough to know better. I'm speaking of the grown men and women in the industry.

L.D.

So do you feel they are leading us in the wrong direction?

Cronyk

"Too late for fakes I see the yard full of snakes." My breakdown of this line is to take someone like Game, only because he is a well-known artist, so his words carry power. So what does he do with it? He stands beside the organization that is killing us and demands we have a civilized conversation with them. He then turns around months later and starts beef with Meek Millz.

What's even crazier is that this action can be found all throughout Hip Hop. Looking on YouTube, I found other artists that only would focus on so-called black on black crime when asked about the subject. It made me wonder, "why are we willing to fight and kill us but be patient with everyone else?"

The Pain I Felt

1. Normally I'd be cool don't ever want to bring no pain

2. normally I Stay Focus don't ever want to play no games

3. but right now I'm really offended cause every time I turn around the industry is telling me to sell out

4. when every new artist song go sell out you gotta make more room for your jailhouse

5. yea straight to the point aiming at the center no time for the jokes

6. the name is cronyk(chronic) no blunts no smoke but you still want to call me dope

7. so what you call me 4 when you knowing that I stand on my principles

8. there ain't dollar sign you can get me 4 I'm kicking old-school game call it give and grow

9. It's sad to see we don't see we got a problem

10. are people still perish for the lack of the knowledge

11. not the type you get in books or the kind you find in college

12. look at the murder rate in the Hood it ain't stopping

13. still see em on the Block let's get it popping

14. too many in jail but the crack Still rocking

15. then turn to the pills that they found in Mom's closet

16. 12 years old and the boy out Robbing

Chorus— the pain I felt it pain forever/ felt like it would rain forever/ everything just came together/ now the king going reign forever/ with the pain I felt it pain forever /felt like it would

rain forever/ everything just came
together /now the king going to reign
forever with the pain
1. I'm a keep my first right and speak
my piece read up so I could teach
2. where we at it ain't cool with me
for all my elders that died for me
3. from slaves to Jim Crow the things
we didn't know when blacks was
gettin beaten off on their backs
4. 1 day Wall Street was black and
then the planes flew through and took
it off the map
5. start telling me what I'm supposed to
do when all this garbage done made it
6. really just peeping the state of hip-
hop n'all Pimpin I Ain't hatin
7. just venting out my frustrations
better that than me to go to catch cases
8.it's life-or-death you got to choose
cause when you pull the trigger

there's no erasing

9. in the pen talking about you mistake him for an enemy that was in the streets

10. they want revenge so they plotting and waiting Clutchin a glock and taking a drink

11. it's a cycle that don't stop the gun a go pop the body go flop somebody called the cops

12. the story of Have Nots Mom and Dad stops the baby done been shot as soon as the heart drops

Chorus- with the pain I feel it pain forever /felt like it'll rain forever/ everything done came together /now the king going to reign forever with the pain (repeat)

L.D.

The pain I felt is touching on some history people are being awakened to recently. So I want to know how this brain of yours looks at it.

Cronyk

I had one word in mind when I first learned of this tragedy, reparations. I here all the time I'm not going to feel bad for something my great great great grandfather did.

So for the sake of this argument let's take slavery off the table and only focus on the 1900's. We were given nothing and built a fully functional blueprint that should have been passed down through our generations. Instead, the blueprint is being destroyed by hatred, fear, and whatever else a person has to have in them to be evil.

L.D.

Ok, so everyone's family that was affected should be paid. I agree.

Cronyk

Yes and no. Yes, everyone's family directly affected should be, but no. I mean all of my cultural was affected.

L.D.

How?

Cronyk

When reading the story, you see that other countries were ready to start trading with them.

Think about this you walk into two different shoe stores. You go to buy a pair of shoes at one store they are $99 at the other $139. The first thought that comes to your mind is the store with the higher price is greedy right.

L.D.

I would think so.

Cronyk

Not always the case. If the owner of the port likes you better, you could get them from him at a price that he might not give me. So for me to make the same profit, I'll have to charge more.

The destruction of that city was a blow to everyone in our communities. We don't have uncles and aunties that can say to us, hey I like your hustle you remind me of me let me help you out. Making it simple they made themselves our middle man. Most of the things bought in this country are now made somewhere else, but for us to get our hands on it, we are at the mercy of culture that has shown unexplainable hatred towards us.

That's why I said, " where we at ain't cool with me for all my elders that died for me," after slavery was abolished, the killing did not stop.

L.D.

That knowledge right there is power. If they paid us one day what would you suggest we do with it?

Cronyk

"The name is Cronyk no blunts no smoke, but you still want

to call me dope, so what you call me fo." Be ourselves no matter what any other nation calls us. We shouldn't try to build like any other culture. We have to find what works for us.

If you don't take it upon yourself to find your history, you will never know it.

A lot of the people that helped to change the face of this country during the 60's are still alive. They remember the morals and values we once held. So why would you get knowledge from a book written by someone that has to give you second-hand information? I make it my business to talk to my elders, and I don't mean just my family. Anytime you see someone with grey hair and wrinkles you should be jumping to go out of your way to give them an ear. It's the job of the generation in the middle to bridge the gap. Listen to gain knowledge from our elders, then turn and pass it to our youth.

Bullets and Bibles

1. I wake up to a new day pray to set my mind free
2. put the garbage behind me
3. still in the hood so easily it can find me
4. so o'clock in doing 40 hours is where you find He
5. but I'm knowing I hate waiting ready to pull me back
6. I must forsake satin so I can stay off on the track
7. my past life was spent chasing Stacks
8. D boys flashing bread trying their best to put me in the Trap
9. bragging about the girls and the trips all over the map
10. what they don't know when they get home they right back in the Trap
11. start doing good checks coming back to back

12. MJ my job got a Bonus that's a check coming back to back to back

13. Now my seeds fresh eating good they not hungry

14. boys looking at me saying that they won't beef

15. grown man to my mama took my brother's OG

16. stay strapped never flashing forever low-key

17. I pray you know I ain't falling for the okie-doke

18. make me mad and I'll be hulk you don't want to be Loki folk

19. my girl talking to me saying baby calm down look around

20. and see how far we come now

21. from standing on the corner with them goons ready to pull a lick

22. to a position broke people want to call Rich

23. so I must keep the peace even if I want to hurt you

24. hit my knees pray to God asking for some virtue so I pray

Chorus- Lord give me serenity to help me change what I can change/ and everything I can't just let me put it in your hands/ I got bullets and bibles(repeat)

1. they got me hot but it's the ending of October

2. they goons when they high but when I pop off they get sober

3. it's another hump day dress for work I gotta get my bread

4. been held back too long so now I got to get ahead

5. my brother went fed that's when I decided to switch

6. he got away clean but his homie decided to snitch

7. that let me know ain't no honor among Thieves

8. so I could either get it right or go and watch my mom grieve boy please

9. believe whatever I do I do a hundred percent pure

10. to feed mine I'll go and shovel cow manure

11. but I don't sleep on threats a coward kill you when you slip.

12. don't make me come hunt you what's in this clip will eat through a brick

13. go call your click both hands on this Chopper pimp tightly gripped

14. and I won't miss so come cross this line and you will be missed

15. but I must keep the peace even if I won't hurt you

16. hit my knees pray to God asking for some virtue so I pray

Chorus- Lord give me serenity help me change what I can change/ and everything I can't just let me put it in your hands/ I got bullets and bibles(repeat)

Now I got scriptures and bible and I got tips for survival
And plus I got them hollow tips and all my niggas with rifles
 But it don't matter what you pick big Blitz is besides you
And plus I'm down to ride on fools but first let me just guide you
You know how your pride do how quickly it can blind you
I wasn't sent to stop you only simply remind
That vengance is mine thus said the Lord of the heavens
And don't forget proverbs 18 and verse 7 Where God instructs
 us a fools mouth is destruction and his lips are the snare for his soul
so behold we were all given this free will to make our own decision
but the road to hell is paved with good intention
when trigger fingers get to itching and tempers start to flair
beware that's just the devil in your ear
we all have a cross to bare so when you week just call on me I'll be your Simon of sirene now let us pray

Chorus- Lord give me serenity help me change what I can change/ and everything I can't just let me put it in your hands/ I got bullets and bibles(repeat)

L.D.

Why did you add someone onto this song?

Cronyk:

I was looking for a different point of view. I feel that this song touches on a subject that we all deal with, the battles that we fight within ourselves.

L.D.

What do bullets and bibles mean to you?

187 Blitz

To me, I see Bullets and Bibles from an American point of view, "Give me liberty or give me death."

The saying, "Praise the Lord and pass the ammunition is the same mind state. It's the Yin and Yang, good and evil, we can either go with these words, or we could go with this lead.

Look at it on the level of, do you want to go higher 5th-dimensional thinking or lower 3rd-dimensional thinking in a material realm. We can work with our animal side, or we can go with our man side, which is raised up from the animal side by the Most High. Simply put we can handle this like gentlemen, or we can get into some Gangsta s***.

L.D.

What are some of the battles that you fight within yourself?

Cronyk:

Growth and development are two battles I fight within myself. When you grow up in a particular area, your concept and view on life are based on what you know. The average person lives his/her life in a five-mile radius. We tend to move close to where we work, so everything we do tends to be within that area.

So, when you make a move like going from the inner city to the suburbs, you end up in a different atmosphere. The way you might have solved a dispute or issue in the inner city could be entirely different from the way you may have addressed an issue in the suburbs.

L.D.

How do bullets and Bibles go together?

Cronyk:

The title is about choices. The hardest battle you have is the one within. You have to fight you harder than you fight anyone.

"I wake up to a new day pray to set my mind free, put the garbage behind me." Every time you get out of bed, you start the fight over.

L.D.

With the current situation of our culture, which one would you apply?

187 Blitz

It depends on which type of person you encounter to make that a necessary reality. You have some people you can link up with and have a conversation with them. You can have a misunderstanding, yet still, take it to the word. The simple level of I am my brother's keeper or love thy neighbor as you love yourself. Basically, can we build, or can we destroy?

My acronym for God is generator operator destroy. Are you going to be the generator, the operator, or the destroyer?

With that in mind, your choice sometimes comes down to, do I have an adversary in front of me, or do I have a foe in front of me?

L.D.

So you will use bullets for yourself?

Cronyk:

Yes, you should kill the parts of you that are counterproductive to your future. You could bypass a lot of problems by getting rid of youthful pride. "But I must keep the peace even if I want to hurt you." Once again you (I) becomes your enemy.

L.D.

Ok if you are using the bullets positively. What are you doing with the Bible?

Cronyk:

One of the benefits to reading it is you will obtain knowledge to build a functional foundation.

L.D.

That changes it from a self-evaluation or a reflection that helps you. To contemplation with the power to establish new guidelines for how we interact.

Cronyk:

Isn't that what we do when we better ourselves? "From standing on the corner with the goons ready to pull a lick, to position broke people want to call rich."

The people around that see you grow are given hope. The entire culture of hip hop is thriving off of this idea. We love to see one of us at the top.

L.D.

In your verse, you sound like the voice of reason. What reasoning would you give to the culture, because the book is speaking of where we are right now and the state we're in so what advice would you give?

187 Blitz

I'll go back to the verse where I stated, "Proverbs 18 verse 7 where God instructs us a Fool's mouth is his destruction and its slips are a snare for his soul" In breaking it down let me ask, have you ever said something and regretted it right after you said it?

Take a relationship that you were in at one time, whether it was romantic or a business partnership, somewhere along the line, something slick got said that destroyed that connection.

Again, we visit that Generator Operator Destroyer (God). The older people used to say, "loose lips sink ships." Before you speak or act on a situation, you should think.

An example of that today is, looking at a social media site, you see people just throw their feelings out there without even thinking about repercussions. That's a speech lead by emotions, instead of thought-out, logical conversation or well-articulated speech.

How many times have you said something, and somebody took it the wrong way? Did they take it the wrong way because you said it in a way for them to become offended, or did you use the most beneficial, powerful, explanatory words you know?

Everyone knows how to talk, but we don't know how to communicate with one another. If we learn how to communicate, then we'll have a communion (common union). Then, we can have a conversation together and build and once again we can generate.

L.D.

I love the fact that both of you have stated that being there for your fellow man is important because it is. The vibe that I'm getting from the conversation resonates in a tone that will build a monumental structure. So my question is how do we get more men thinking this way?

Cronyk

They honestly don't have a choice. The way I see it is there is a war going on in front of us all. No matter how you try to duck it or outrun it, battles are fought every day. Soon and very soon you have to pick a side. Not knowing where you stand is as dangerous as blindly walking through a minefield. When you take into action without thought, you are a hindrance to yourself and those you love.

Wait, before you up and choose a side I hope you take everything into account. Most importantly find out who is your enemy and why are you fighting? Knowledge is very powerful. Having it can equip you with the tools to vanquish your enemy, and not having it could mean your demise.

From the overwhelming number of poverty stricken men being harmed by males in the same bondage shows our enemy has eluded us. Our ancestors were hung by people the natives called pale face, but that doesn't make their children my enemy. Just like Caucasian women were beaten and killed along side of freedom riders, but that doesn't make their offspring my friend.

Deeds of the hand will not always show you a man's real intent, but drunken lips will confess what the heart is thinking. All you have to do is listen.

Boastfully our enemy has shown pictures of our brother's blood running from our hands, glorified as art. Systematically removing my elder men from the round table, leaving my platoon unguided. So I stand ready and willing to fight, but not against my brother; because you are not my enemy.

Sanity

1. I'm tired of all of this fakeness so I aint finna participate

2. grabbed the pen to rock this beat cuz man I really got something to say

3. I'm going to keep it plain make it blunt it's (Cronyk)chronic man I'm never Folding Up

4. Just Like a Pillor forever holding up and for the trill og's I'm showing up

5. I've been sitting back and been watching what I seen done made me sick

6. kids kill themselves to get rich and you ain't never sold no brick

7. you ain't never sold no hard the life you live was just made up

8. straight A's in school took up vocab to find a way to come play us

9. reciting lines that was written by Scarface ball and MJG

10. I know the real and seen the trill so you ain't finna come play me

11. tell em get money and bank it floss out with you drinking

12. but forget to teach them math because if he's nothing you nathing

13. my community they've been raping she crying screaming for the saving

14. in fear trembling shaking with murder off they get away with

15. I'm still repping that dirty south clean dressin that dirty mouth

16. door closed and all the lames kicked out and I'm just the broom for this dirty house so let's go

Chorus— all I'm trying to do is keep my sanity (repeat 4 times)

1. mama in the kitchen crying baby boy just got shot

2. on the news they say the killer was masked up and had to glocks

3. 2 hours ago he was busting riding around with his posse

4. turning up getting hype to that rap dude from Degrassi

5. but he ain't never bust no shots He ani't never pop no slugs

6. every time beef came his way he quickly tucked them up

7. but he ain't the only one living fake on TV that's playing hard

8. because Pimp dead but before he died he pulled like a whole lot of cards

9. selling garbage to these babies things you wouldn't let your kids do

10. say that you got love for the block but when the last time you fell through

11. only given half of the game like cars women and all the bread
12. forget to tell the true stories bout all the goons in jail and dead
13. my community they been raping and she crying screaming for the saving
14. in fear trembling shaking with murder off they get away with
15. I'm still repping that dirty south clean dressing that dirty mouth
16. door closed and the lames kicked out and I'm just a broom for this dirty house so let's go
Chorus— all I'm trying to do is keep my sanity (repeat)

L.D.

Oh wow, you went at rap in a way I haven't heard most rappers do. Why?

Cronyk

Somehow hip hop aka rap stopped rapping. Beats became more important than what was said. I catch myself putting logic to this recent debate between legends and newcomers. Music following the trend of great beats, catchy hooks, and nonsense jargon is not rap. The definition of rap is 1. Strike with a series of rapid audible blows, especially to attract attention. 2. Talk or chat in an easy and familiar manner. In Layman's terms, it means to have a conversation, and no one can talk with you when you are mumbling.

L.D.

So you don't think riding a groove is the same as being an MC?

Cronyk

I would never be caught saying they are the same. The art of MCing was created as a way to inform while entertaining the people. Riding a beat is only entertainment.

See, our neighborhoods had all the ingredients to be great, not until the over excessive push of negative perception displayed in the industry did they become self-imploding.

L.D.

Ok, so you're answering the age old question: Does life imitate art?

Cronyk

"Mama in the kitchen crying baby boy just got shot, on the new, they say the killer was masked up with two glocks. 2 hours ago he was bustin riding around with his posse, turning up getting hype to that rap dude from Degrassi." Those lines are me painting a picture of life that happens way too often.

L.D.

Drake is at the top of the game. Is this a shot for notoriety, or something else?

Cronyk

"He ain't the only one living fake on TV, playing hard cause Pimp dead, but before he died, he pulled like a whole lot of cards." It's not an issue with him. It's a problem with everybody portraying negativity in the industry.

L.D.

That makes a lot of sense. The painter has control over the painting he paints. Anyone reading this can tell that you are bothered by this very much, why?

Cronyk

We have had every lie propitiated on us as men possible. From the lies of all crime are done by the black community, to keep your white daughters away from those black males they are animals wanting to rape them.

So answer me this, why on God's green earth would you go and make up these fairytale gangster images of yourselves? The most sickening part of it all is the rappers that portray this vision of themselves are far from it. Most are only given the credit for not learning from their mistakes, so they will surely do it again. Not being mature enough to know that you have a significant influence on the generation behind you.

So that one night of getting angry at the club that turns into a fight plastered all over the news will eventually add up to countless lives lost to death or prison.

We have the opportunity to make the world hear and see whatever we want. Hip Hop became its own news broadcast, and at the height of its power what do we show? The exact angry black men that they said we were.

The old excuse of its art will not be accepted anymore. Personal responsibility has to be taken along with a plan to fix what you have helped destroy. This is just the beginning of a list of demands that I hope the community will start to require before they pledge support to all of you fake, Oscar-deserving artist.

Granny Song

1. Pain pain is a motivator if you let it be
2. First it stops your normal pattern then you breathe (Gotta Move)
3. Crazy how things we don't see can mean so much
4. You can't live without air love you can't touch
5. A blind man can't see so the sun rises he'll never miss
6. But once you're gone he'll forever long for your love your touch your kiss

Chorus- you're my Sunday go to church/ Monday go to work/ please understand me/ you can't forget family/ it hurt so bad I want you back (repeat 2 times) you said I would go far/ sure to be a star/ keep yourself

humble/ you can't forget God/ It hurt
so bad I want you back (repeat 2
times)

1. I went to listen to your last sermon
never let go Gods unchanging hand
2. Nothing is new under the sun you
live now but deaths sure to come
3. Crazy how everybody told me I'll be
okay I think I shut down
4. Honestly I still feel like I'm out of
touch now
5. The things that made me smile to
them I've numbed my soul
6. The world that you made warm now
feels so cold
Chorus- you're my Sunday go to
church/ Monday go to work/ please
understand me/ you can't forget
family/ it hurt so bad I want you
back (repeat 2 times) You said I would

go far/ sure to be a star/ keep yourself
humble you can't forget God/ it hurt
so bad want you back (repeat 2 times)

No one said it would be easy.
But I got to keep going
Keep on trusting
Keep on believing y'all
I got to keep on Keep on keep on keep
on
Chorus- you're my Sunday go to
church/ Monday go to work/ please
understand me/ you can't forget
family/ it hurt so bad I want you
back (repeat 2 times) you said I would
go far/ sure to be a star/ keep yourself
humble you can't forget God/ it hurt
so bad I want you back (repeat 2
times)

L.D.

Let me first say sorry for your loss, and I like that you made a powerful song out of it. You went to church on this song, so I'm assuming Thelma Lue is your grandmother's name.

Cronyk

Thank you, I can say I was a very blessed young man. Growing up, I had three out of four grandparents and both parents who actively contributed to me maturing into a man.

L.D.

That is great! When you are from the inner city, you don't hear that much. It shows up in your conversation.

Cronyk

I have started to recognize it more lately. A lot of the props I get for being wise is just knowledge passing through me. My elders gave me a hunger for information, so when most kids were trying to get away from their elders, I would sit up under mine. That's why I give that advice because I know it works. "You're my Sunday go to church Monday go to work" was my childhood. I remember hearing her say all of the time if a man doesn't work, he doesn't eat.

The Sunday go to church was more than the church; it was the foundation of our family. After service, our entire family aunts, uncles, and cousins would eat together.

The deacons and ushers were very strict, and of course, as children, we didn't like it, but it has helped in many aspects of my adult life. Everything surrounding that building became a cornerstone for the structure I craved.

L.D.

I like that you showed your personal pain in this song. So many artists only write what they see, not allowing their fans into personal feelings.

Cronyk

I can understand why. Some people aren't very kind. So if they opened up and someone used it to take a shot at them, it could get ugly. Honestly, I've never paid attention to what people say. If you do, you'll find yourself not doing anything. That's something I watched her do every day of her life. If she had something to say she just said it, and if something needed to get done, she just did it.

L.D.

What would you say she taught you that you'd never forget?

Cronyk

Love! She had a heart that made her help everyone. It wasn't to gloat either. You know how some people do things so they can hold it over your head. She did it, and no one would know.

Also, she never stopped talking to the youth. When I watched a lot of elders stop communicating with young people, she didn't. Every breath she had, she gave to trying to help those that couldn't help themselves.

L.D.

Sounds like a great woman that you truly miss.

Cronyk

She is and will be for a long time.

My GOD

1 - If you Made it this far then you know you don't talk to no square box

2 - been on the fence so long I can tell you that hells hot

3 - most of my friends seen the pen we all used to sell rocks

4 - still buying straps now so they think that I'm shell-shocked

5 - tried to live my life by all of their rules

6 - so what you do when you find out really man it ain't true

7 - make your move or try to blind your whole vision

8 - take your jems and try to make a prism to shed light on a religion

9 - so I went and read the book for myself

10-we perish for the lack of knowledge boy and what they pull is just theft

11-creating the problems for death then telling us it's our self

12-like they had was missing when we got to Tripping yeah we had the guns but they gave ammunition

13-Steiwee went to the pen I'm staying with Granny in the bricks

14-hoping to get my life right time was spent in the scripts

15-it was a whole 180 flip from being the one to want to go the hardest

16-to understanding to bend my knees and give thanks to my Lord and God man

Chorus- I'm a believer do you believe I'm a believer/ believe in love believe

in yourself I'm a believe in God God I
believe in you

1 -It seems like problem start building
up everything got bigger

2 -when I decided from my sins I need
to be delivered

3 -change ain't easy but it will come
just know you not to picker

4 -of time when it shines and tells you
to please move a little bit quicker

5 -but I didn't heed kept denying my
path can't lie about that

6 -I was trying to do me but I never lost
sight it kept coming right back

7 -one night I was 15 riding around
with my og's

8 -we was bumping 8 -ball MJ and
blowing on some of that ooh we

9 - in the review I seeing flashing lights didn't flexed didn't bend didn't jump

10 - threw the bag of grass off in my mouth and had a TEC-9 locked in the trunk

11 - I was young and dumb or either nuts because I wasn't right

12 - it was 1:15 I'm a minor in my face a flashlight

13 - hand him my permit kept it cool stay calm

14 - gunshots rang out he threw it back and told me to head home

15 - I ain't glorifying my pass in the midst of this song

16 - just trying to say my God had me in the mist of my wrong

Chorus- I'm a believer do you believe I'm a believer/ believe in love believe

yourself I'm a believe in God God I
believe in you

L.D.

Tell me about this song. What is the meaning of the song?

Cronyk

This song is about scripture coming to life. It's about my path and relationship with God.

L.D.

So what would you say to someone like myself that doesn't understand the Bible?

Cronyk

I would tell you to pray for understanding and continue reading. The first time I read the bible, I became lost. My second time around, I began to understand the bible's teachings.

Everything is difficult the first time you do it. After a while, it gets easier.

L.D.

Do you believe the pictures of Jesus are correct?

Cronyk

I have a question. Have you ever heard anyone read a scripture that describes Jesus the way pictures depict him?

You see, we catch ourselves listening to others opinions describing his features. They want to paint a picture depicting someone that society may deem appealing.

I'll be the first to tell you once I read the bible, I stopped believing in religion.

L.D

What do you mean you stopped believing in religion?

Cronyk

I don't believe in religion. The bible was around centuries before Christianity, right? It is difficult to separate the two. People believe that if you believe in the bible, it automatically means you are a Christian. That word isn't even in the bible. The word is God inspired. Religion is MAN's interpretation of what they learn from the Bible.

L.D.

So you are telling me you have read the Bible from front to back?

Cronyk

"Stewee went to the pen I'm staying with granny in the brick, hoping to get my life right, so time was spent in the script."

During the summer, when I was 19, I sat in the house and read the Bible from Revelations to Revelations.

L.D.

Isn't that the end? Everyone always says that book of the Bible scares them.

Cronyk

Yes, but that's how I started. I quickly learned most of the scriptures we hear in church people take out of context. We can put the word, to action, and resolve a lot of the issues that we face.

L.D.

Ok, now you have me interested. Give me examples.

Cronyk

The crazy part is we have already done this in our culture we just lost it. Check this
Matthew 18:21-22

21 Then came Peter to him, and said, Lord, how often shall my brother sin against me, and I forgive him? until seven times?

22 Jesus saith unto him, I say not unto thee, until seven times: but, until seventy times seven.
The Bible verse is very important; Do you remember when I told you before the system stepped in, black on black crime didn't exist? Now we kill each other over shoes, cars, women, and just simple jealousy. Could you imagine how many people would be alive if we just would forgive seventy times seven?

L.D.

If you understand the bible, why are you not a gospel rapper? Truly speaking I've been to church and have yet to be taught that.

Cronyk

Because titles are boxes, they only close you in. I believe, and I openly speak. It goes deeper, in churches, people tell you to tithe, but they do not break down what is the purpose of the money collected.

Deuteronomy 14 verse 28:29 says

28 At the end of three years thou shalt bring forth all the tithe of thine increase the same year, and shalt lay *it* up within thy gates:

29 And the Levite, (because he hath no part nor inheritance with thee,) and the stranger, and the fatherless, and the widow, which *are* within thy gates, shall come, and shall eat and be satisfied; that the LORD thy God may bless thee in all the work of thine hand which thou doesn't.

This verse teaches us how we gained even when they gave us scraps. We took care of each other, spent our money with each other first. The days of Martin, Malcolm, and The Panthers were all about this teaching, and we can see it worked. The Harlem Renaissance also can be used to teach us about the power we hold when we work together. My grandmother taught me that during black people's economic success they would circulate 1 dollar in their community seven times before they let it leave.

L.D.

Just curious what would that help?

Cronyk

The main problem surrounding every issue at hand is the way system chooses to solve problems. Look at every culture in the world as children, what worked with your daughter might not work with your son. They have tailored things in a way that specifically helps them. And how you may ask? True capital. He who holds the money makes the rules, so we need to hold our own.

L.D.

So, you are telling me you got all of this from the Bible?

Cronyk

Yes it says plain as day
<u>Deuteronomy 24:10</u>
When thou dost lend thy brother anything, thou shalt not go
into his house to fetch his pledge.

Now isn't that what the system does to us. You can borrow
food stamps as long as you promise you won't try to keep
your family together.

Our system didn't do that to us. The Black Panthers created
the WIC program, and this program didn't ask for us to
separate our families. The only way we'll have any control
over what our future looks like is to get back to what built us.

I don't want equality; I want to be left alone. Let us build and
not be bothered; this will solve everyone's problems. They
say our children are out of control and need to stop killing
each other and I agree. So I say if your culture doesn't want to
whip your child, that's for you. We believe in spare the rod
spoil the child, but you want to lock us up. They say I'm tired
of giving them our money, once again I agree. I can't stand the
rules that come with your money.

The only thing I've ever wondered is, why us? The Asian, the
Indians from India, Middle Eastern from Pakistan or any other
part of the Middle East, and Africans are all left alone to build
in America. But, if we lay a brick to start a foundation, here
comes that dreadful, hateful, corrupted people we all pay to
uphold justice.

L.D.

A lot of people don't step up to the forefront for the very reasons you mentioned. Now with some leaders of new black movements are killed suspiciously, are you scared to step up?

Cronyk

"Not glorifying my past in the midst of this song, just telling you my God had me in the midst of my wrong." If he had me then, he has me now.

The Interview (written by Chauncey Smith Jr. Track by Flawless)

The Product Feat. Ian (written by Chauncey Smith Jr. Track by Flawless)

Trust Issues Feat. Don Dadda Da Gr8 (written by Chauncey Smith Jr. Track by Dizzee Beats)

Every Time (written by Chauncey Smith Jr. Track by Vybe Beatz)

Hello Officer (written by Chauncey Smith Jr. Track by Scott Supreme)

Paradise (written by Chauncey Smith Jr. and Tom Davids Track by Tom Davids)

Breakfast Feat. Q (written by Chauncey Smith Jr. Track by Superstar O)

Stretch Greys Feat. Deremus Jones (written by Chauncey Smith Jr. Track by Zone Beats)

Leave Me Alone Feat. Oshea, Lil D, Don Dadda Da Gr8 (written by Chauncey Smith Jr., Oshea Stewart, Don Williams Jr., and Don Williams Sr. Track by Dizzee Beats)

This That Track (written by Chauncey Smith Jr. Track by Dizzee Beats)

Bullets and Bibles (written by Chauncey Smith Jr. and 187 Blitz Track by Dizzee Beats)

The Pain I Felt (written by Chauncey Smith Jr. Track by Dizzee Beats)

Sanity Feat. Deremus Jones (written by Chauncey Smith Jr. Track by Matthew primetime Martin)

Thelma Lue Feat. Marcus Fuller and Deremus Jones (written by Chauncey Smith Jr., Marcus Filler, and Deremus Jones Track by Tone Jonez)

My GOD Feat. Ian (written by Chauncey Smith Jr. and Rico McClean produced by Scott Supreme)

All songs recorded and mixed by Rico McClean, AMG Studios, Iso and mastered by Reavis Mitchell